D1088993

LOVE

LOVE

An Illustrated Treasury

Compiled by Michelle Lovriç

COURAGE BOOKS

an imprint of
RUNNING PRESS
Philadelphia, Pennsylvania

Copyright © 1992 by Royle Publications Limited
                    Royle Publications,
                    Royle House,
                    Wenlock Road,
                    London N1 7ST
                    England
Concept developed by Michelle Lovric
                    Publishing Consultant
                    3 Church Street
                    Bath Avon BA1 1NL
                    England
Compilation and introduction copyright © 1992 Michelle
Lovric.

Printed in Hong Kong. All rights reserved under the Pan-
American and International Copyright Conventions.

This book may not be reproduced in whole or in part in any
form or by any means, electronic or mechanical, including
photocopying, recording, or by any information storage and
retrieval system now known or hereafter invented, without
written permission from the publisher.

Canadian representatives: General Publishing Co., Ltd.,
30 Lesmill Road, Don Mills, Ontario M3B 2T6.

9 8 7 6 5 4 3 2
Digit on the right indicates the number of this printing.

Library of Congress Cataloging-in-Publication Number 91–58802
ISBN 1–56138–121–7
Cover design by Toby Schmidt
Text edited by Cynthia L. Gitter
Interior design by Nancy Loggins
Typography by Commcor Communications Corporation,
Philadelphia, Pennsylvania

Published by Courage Books, an imprint of
Running Press Book Publishers
125 South Twenty-second Street
Philadelphia, Pennsylvania 19103

*I*NTRODUCTION

THE NEED TO EXPRESS AND SHARE THE TURBULENT JOYS OF LOVE HAS BEEN COMMON TO ALL AGES AND ALL CULTURES. EVERY GENERATION HAS PRODUCED ITS OWN ELOQUENT PHILOSOPHERS WHO CHAMPION THE CAUSE OF LOVE WITH WORDS OF FINE PROSE, POETRY, AND WIT.

LOVE ITSELF HAS ITS OWN MYSTERIOUS SEQUENCE, FROM SWEET SEDUCTION TO FULL-FLAVORED PASSION, FROM THE FEVER OF DESIRE TO THE CHILL OF REJECTION, FROM THE PROLOGUE OF COURTSHIP TO THE CENTRAL ACT OF MARRIAGE. LOVE ROUNDS OUR EXPERIENCE WITH AN ABILITY TO LAUGH AT OURSELVES, ITS FOOLS.

JUST AS LOVE PROPELS THE WRITER, IT ALSO SPURS THE ARTIST. THE SAME METAPHORS FOR LOVE— FLOWERS, THE SEA, THE SEASONS—ARE APPROPRIATED BY BOTH POET AND PAINTER. IN THIS SELECTION THERE IS GOOD REASON FOR THE HARMONY OF TEXT AND IMAGE: THE ILLUSTRATIONS ARE CHOSEN FROM THE VAST ARCHIVES OF ROYLE PUBLICATIONS LIMITED, WHICH HAS BEEN SELECTING AND COMMISSIONING FINE ARTWORK FOR GREETING CARDS FOR NEARLY 50 YEARS.

All,
everything
that I
understand,
I understand
only because
I love.

LEO TOLSTOY (1828–1910)
RUSSIAN WRITER

seven

Love is an

act of

endless

forgiveness,

a tender

look which

becomes a

habit.

PETER USTINOV, B. 1921
ENGLISH ACTOR AND WRITER

*L*OVE DEMANDS ALL AND HAS A RIGHT TO IT.

Ludwig von Beethoven (1770–1827)
German composer

LOVE IS THE STATE IN WHICH MAN SEES THINGS
MOST WIDELY DIFFERENT FROM WHAT THEY ARE.

Friedrich Wilhelm Nietzsche (1844–1900)
German philosopher

LOVE IS LAK THE SEA. IT'S A MOVIN'

THING, BUT STILL AND ALL, IT TAKES ITS

SHAPE FROM DE SHORE IT MEETS, AND IT'S

DIFFERENT WITH EVERY SHORE.

Zora Neale Hurston (1901–1960)
American writer

The heart of another is a dark forest, always,

no matter how close it has been to one's own.

WILLA CATHER (1873–1947)
AMERICAN WRITER

To love and win is the best thing; to love and lose, the next best.

WILLIAM MAKEPEACE THACKERAY (1811–1863)
ENGLISH WRITER

Love

conquers

all things,

except

poverty

and

toothache.

MAE WEST (1892–1980)
AMERICAN ACTRESS

*L*ove is a crutch, that's all, and there isn't any one of us that doesn't need a crutch.

LOVE,
IT IS SAID,
IS BLIND;
BUT LOVE IS
NOT BLIND.
IT IS AN
EXTRA EYE
WHICH
SHOWS US
WHAT IS MOST
WORTHY OF
REGARD.

J. M. Barrie (1860–1937)
Scottish writer

The

heart

has its

reasons

which

reason

knows

nothing of.

BLAISE PASCAL (1623–1662)
FRENCH WRITER

LOVE IZ LIKE THE MEAZLES; WE KANT HAVE IT BAD BUT ONST, AND THE LATER IN LIFE WE HAVE IT THE TUFFER IT GOES WITH US.

Josh Billings (1818–1885),
American humorist

AND I WOULD LOVE YOU ALL THE DAY,

EVERY NIGHT WOULD KISS AND PLAY,

IF WITH ME YOU'D FONDLY STRAY

OVER THE HILLS AND FAR AWAY.

John Gay (1688–1732)
English poet

*P*ermit me voyage, love, into

your hands. . . .

HART CRANE (1899–1932)
AMERICAN POET

ANY TIME
THAT IS NOT SPENT
ON LOVE IS
WASTED.

Torquato Tasso (1544–1595)
Italian poet

Love begets love. This torment is my joy.

THEODORE ROETHKE (1908–1963)
AMERICAN POET

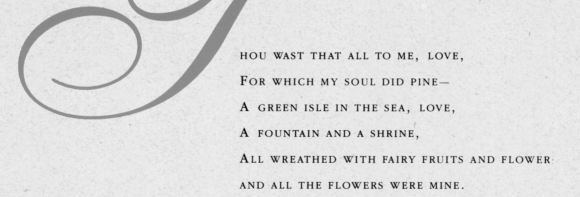

THOU WAST THAT ALL TO ME, LOVE,

FOR WHICH MY SOUL DID PINE—

A GREEN ISLE IN THE SEA, LOVE,

A FOUNTAIN AND A SHRINE,

ALL WREATHED WITH FAIRY FRUITS AND FLOWER

AND ALL THE FLOWERS WERE MINE.

Edgar Allan Poe (1809–1849)
American writer

You,

Beloved,

who are

all the

gardens I

have ever

gazed at,

longing.

RAINER MARIA RILKE (1875–1926)
AUSTRIAN POET

IN THE SILENCE OF NIGHT I HAVE OFTEN WISHED FOR JUST A FEW WORDS OF LOVE FROM ONE MAN, RATHER THAN THE APPLAUSE OF THOUSANDS OF PEOPLE.

Judy Garland (1922–1969)
American actress

SEPARATENESS IS SWEET BUT CONNECTION WITH SOMEONE OUTSIDE YOURSELF IS SURELY SWEETER.

JUDITH VIORST, B. 1931
AMERICAN WRITER

My

dream

soul

exists

only

for

you.

YUAN CHEN (779–831)
CHINESE POET

AND ALL HER FACE WAS HONEY TO MY MOUTH,

AND ALL HER BODY PASTURE TO MINE EYES.

Algernon Swinburne (1837–1909)
English poet

Don't you think I was
made for you?
I feel like you
had me ordered
—and I was delivered to you—
to be worn—
I want you to wear me,
like a watch-charm
or a button hole bouquet—
to the world.

ZELDA FITZGERALD (1900–1948)
AMERICAN WRITER

I HAVE SPREAD MY DREAMS
UNDER YOUR FEET;
TREAD SOFTLY, BECAUSE YOU TREAD
ON MY DREAMS.

William Butler Yeats (1865–1939)
Irish poet

THOU ART

TO ME A

DELICIOUS

TORMENT.

Ralph Waldo Emerson (1803–1882)
American writer

*J*seem to have loved you in numberless forms, numberless times,
In life after life, in age after age forever.

RABINDRATH TAGORE (1861–1941)
INDIAN WRITER

Since you went away

Gold and green hairpins have lost their glint.

LIU CHUN (430–464)
CHINESE POET

THOSE WHOM WE CAN LOVE, WE CAN
HATE; TO OTHERS WE ARE INDIFFERENT.

Henry David Thoreau (1817–1862)
American writer

am jealous of the

perfumed air of night

That from this garden

climbs to kiss thy lips.

HENRY WADSWORTH LONGFELLOW (1807–1882)
AMERICAN POET

THE SIMPLE LACK OF HER IS MORE TO ME

THAN OTHERS' PRESENCE.

Edward Thomas (1878–1917)
English poet

Everyone has experienced that truth: that

love, like a running brook, is disregarded,

taken for granted; but when the brook freezes

over, then people begin to remember how it

was when it ran, and they want it to run again.

KAHLIL GIBRAN (1883–1931)
LEBANESE POET

NLY

IF YOU BARTERED

YOUR HEART

FOR MINE

WOULD YOU KNOW

HOW MUCH

I MISS YOU!

Ku Hsiung, c. 928
Chinese poet

LIFE IS STREWN WITH THESE MIRACLES FOR WHICH PEOPLE WHO LOVE CAN ALWAYS HOPE.

Marcel Proust (1871–1922)
French writer

Farewell!

thou art

too dear

for my

possessing.

WILLIAM SHAKESPEARE (1564–1616)
ENGLISH DRAMATIST

When I loved you, I can't but allow

I had many an exquisite minute;

But the scorn that I feel for you now

Hath even more luxury in it!

Thus, whether we're on or we're off,

Some witchery seems to await you;

To love you is pleasant enough,

But oh! 'tis delicious to hate you!

THOMAS MOORE (1779–1852)
IRISH POET

MY SAD HEART FOAMS AT THE STERN.

Arthur Rimbaud (1854–1891)
French poet

THIS IS THE CROWN AND BLESSING OF MY LIFE,

THE MUCH LOVED HUSBAND OF A HAPPY WIFE;

TO HIM WHOSE CONSTANT PASSION FOUND THE ART

TO WIN A STUBBORN AND UNGRATEFUL HEART,

AND TO THE WORLD BY TENDEREST PROOF DISCOVERS

THEY ERR, WHO SAY THAT HUSBANDS CAN'T BE LOVERS.

Anne, Countess of Winchilsea (1661–1720)
English poet

It's not that I suffer
for want of food,
True sorrow comes
from feelings starved.
I sit down
in tense abstraction,
And imagine
your radiant face.

HSU KAN (171–214)
CHINESE POET

WEDLOCK—THE DEEP, DEEP PEACE OF
THE DOUBLE BED AFTER THE HURLY-BURLY
OF THE CHAISE-LONGUE.

Beatrice Tanner (1865–1940)
British actress

A lady's
imagination
is very rapid;
it jumps from
admiration
to love,
and from
love
to matrimony,
in a
moment.

JANE AUSTEN (1775–1817)
ENGLISH WRITER

A man in the house is worth
two in the street.

MAE WEST (1892–1980)
AMERICAN ACTRESS

THERE IS NO MORE LOVELY, FRIENDLY, OR CHARMING RELATIONSHIP, COMMUNION,
OR COMPANY THAN A GOOD MARRIAGE.

Martin Luther (1483–1546)
German reformer

The ring, so worn as you behold,

So thin, so pale, is yet of gold.

The passion such it was to prove:

Worn with life's care, love yet was love.

GEORGE CRABBE (1754–1832)
ENGLISH POET AND CLERIC

ILLUSTRATION ACKNOWLEDGMENTS

COVER: *Mixed Roses and Nasturtiums,* Margaretta Rosenboom

TITLE PAGE: *Bal à Bougival* (detail), Pierre Auguste Renoir (Courtesy The Museum of Fine Arts, Boston)

p.7: *A Still Life of Roses,* Johann Laurents Jensen (Courtesy Fine Art Photographic Library Ltd.)

p.9: *At the End of the Garden,* Vernon Ward

p.13: *Mixed Roses and Nasturtiums,* Margaretta Rosenboom

p.15: *The Holy Family with the Infant St. John,* Domenico Zampieri (Domenichino) (Courtesy Devonshire Collection, Chatsworth)

p.16: *Little Speedwell, Darling Blue,* Sir John Everett Millais (Courtesy National Museums and Galleries on Merseyside—Lady Lever Art Gallery)

p.18: *Small Talk,* Eugene de Blaas